Pam Wedgwood's
RecorderWorld
Ensemble

by PAM WEDGWOOD

illustrations by DREW HILLIER

© 2005 by Faber Music Ltd
First published in 2005 by Faber Music Ltd
3 Queen Square London WC1N 3AU
Cover by Shireen Nathoo design
Music processed by MusicSet 2000
Printed in England by Caligraving Ltd
All rights reserved

ISBN 0-571-52381-1

To buy Faber Music publications or to find out about the full range of titles
available please contact your local music retailer or Faber Music sales enquiries:

Faber Music Limited, Burnt Mill, Elizabeth Way, Harlow, CM20 2HX England
Tel: +44 (0)1279 82 89 82   Fax: +44 (0)1279 82 89 83
sales@fabermusic.com   fabermusic.com

FABER *ff* MUSIC

Monday morning

Play this when you reach stage 2

Pam Wedgwood

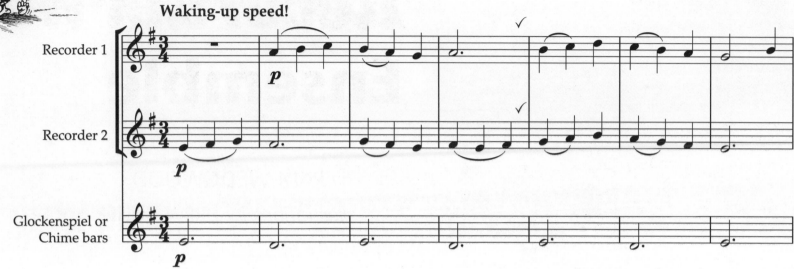

The stick dance

Play this when you reach stage 4

Praetorius
arr. Wedgwood

3

Daisy, Daisy

Play this when you reach stage 4

Traditional
arr. Wedgwood

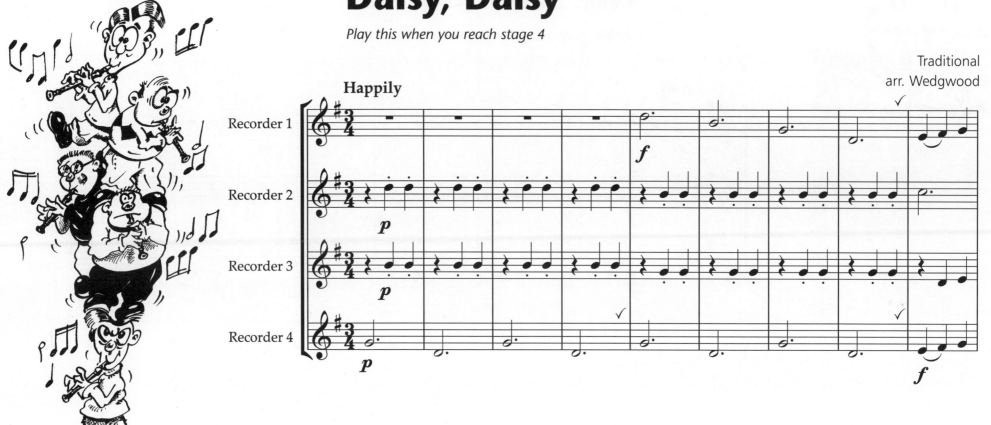

Bransle

Play this when you reach stage 4

Gervaise
arr. Wedgwood

PERCUSSION BOX

Tambourine

Drum

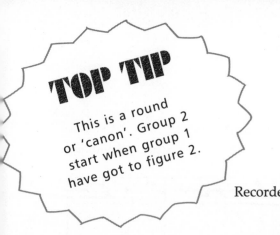

TOP TIP

This is a round or 'canon'. Group 2 start when group 1 have got to figure 2.

Follow the leader †

Play this when you reach stage 6

Purcell
arr. Wedgwood

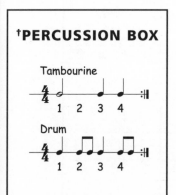

†**PERCUSSION BOX**

Tambourine

Drum

Jogging along

Play this when you reach stage 7

Pam Wedgwood

Steadily

7

Be-bop-a-lu-la

Play this when you reach stage 7

Medium rock 'n' roll

Pam Wedgwood

FINE

D. C. al Fine

Cool dude

Play this when you reach stage 10

Pam Wedgwood

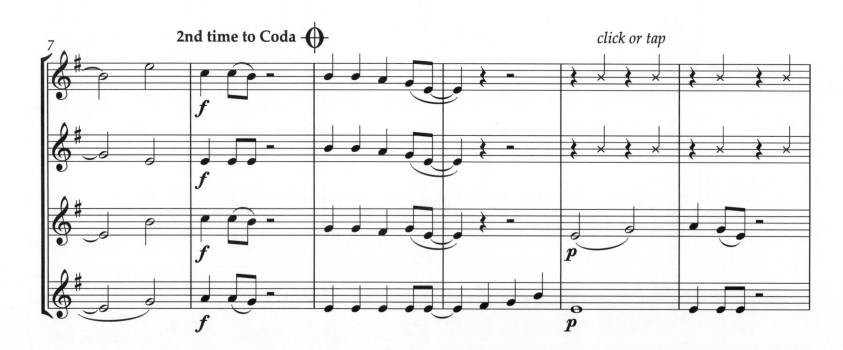

Summer is icumen in

Play this when you reach stage 12

Traditional
arr. Wedgwood

Springtime *from* Symphony No. 6, 'Pastoral'

Play this when you reach stage 13

Beethoven
arr. Wedgwood

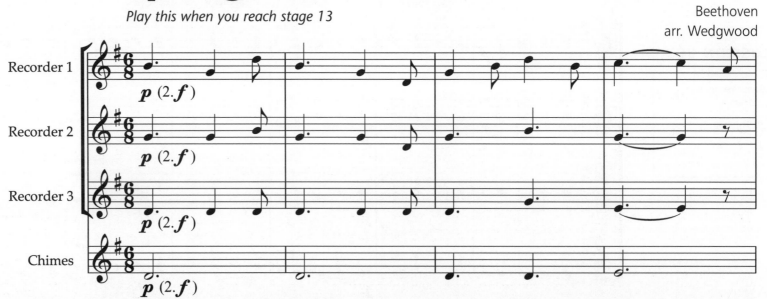

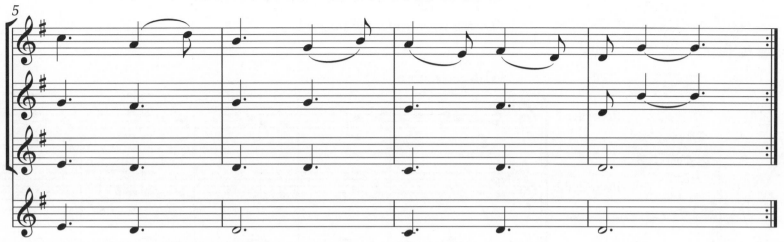

It's Springtime!

Chant

Play this when you reach stage 15

Pam Wedgwood

Sadly

Recorder 1

Recorder 2

Recorder 3

Spaghetti samba

Play this when you reach stage 15

With movement

Pam Wedgwood

PERCUSSION BOX

Fanfare

Play this when you reach stage 15

Pam Wedgwood

With a good flourish!

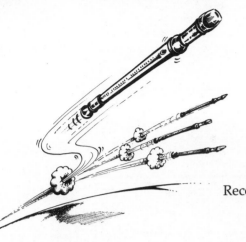

FINE

D. C. al Fine